The Selfish Heart

By Mark Henry Scanlon

Introduction

This book is a journey of meditations, leading you step by step into deeper communion with God. Each meditation is designed to guide you through the mystery of the Trinity, not just as a concept, but as a lived experience. As you read and reflect, open your heart to the path laid before you. Each meditation focuses on a specific person of the Trinity. You will:

- Walk with the Son in His sacrifice and experience the depth of His love for us.
- Meet with the Spirit and learn to know Him.
- Return home to the Father, with the Spirit, by the narrow path of the Son, that leads to eternal communion with Him.

While this journey is not a literal one, as we can only fully meet the Father at the end of our lives, it helps us deepen our connection with the Spirit and set our hearts on the ultimate goal: to return home to the Father, in the Spirit, by walking in the steps of the Son.

What is Imaginative Prayer?

Imaginative prayer is a form of mental prayer that deepens our meditation and allows us to experience Scripture in a personal and transformative way. This method has its roots in the spiritual exercises of St. Ignatius of Loyola, with the goal of placing ourselves within the text. By engaging our senses, we make the scene as real and vivid as possible, moving beyond a mere intellectual understanding to engage the heart and emotions, drawing us closer to God.

Why it is Important?

Many of us read Scripture but feel distant from the text, as if it belongs to another time and place. We learn about Jesus, through the Gospels what he did and through modern science the world he was living in, but it is difficult to gain a deeper and more personal connection. Which as Christians is the goal, to become too close to Christ we become more Christ like. Imaginative prayer changes that. It brings Scripture to life, making it a living, breathing reality to be experienced and allowed to change us. Instead of just reading about Christ, you will walk with Him, suffer with Him, and be embraced by His love. This transforms not only how you pray but how you see God in your daily life. This method deepens our spiritual life, cultivates a more profound love for Christ, and transforms the way we see Him working in our daily experiences.

How This Booklet Will Help You

This booklet is designed to guide you through the practice of imaginative prayer using a structured approach that is accessible to people of all abilities:

- How to prepare for prayer with the right mindset and environment.
- How to engage your imagination and senses.
- Step-by-step guided meditations on the Father, Son, and Holy Spirit.
- Reflection prompts to deepen your experience and relationship with God.

By the end of this journey, you will not only have learned a new way of praying but will also have encountered the love of Christ in a deeply personal and transformative way. Let us embark on this journey together, opening our hearts to the selfless love of God and learning to love Him in return.

The Selfish Heart, the Selfless God

We must learn to love Him, the way He loves us

Opening Prayer

Father, I come before you with an open heart, seeking to understand more deeply, the sacrifice of your Son our Lord Jesus Christ. At times words can feel empty, lacking the chance for a personal encounter with our saviour. Through the power of your most beautiful spirit Lord I ask that you make quiet my thoughts, calm my heart, and lead me into deeper communion with You. Let Your wisdom flow within me, that I may experience the love that lead Jesus to suffer so much for me.

Amen

Philippians 3:10 - *"I want to know Christ, yes, to know the power of his resurrection and participation in his sufferings, becoming like him in his death."*

Guided Meditation on the Passion

Preparing the Mind and Heart

Before we begin, take a moment to focus on your breath. With each inhale and exhale, let go of distractions and allow yourself to fully enter into the meditation. This will help make the meditation on the Passion more vivid, pulling you away from the external world and fully into the presence of Christ. This initial part can last for a few minutes.

Entering the Scene

You are in Jerusalem. Crowds have gathered along the roads leading to Golgotha, a mixture of angry jeers and cries of despair fill the air. You stand at the front of the crowd, watching the events unfold. The scent of the people around you, dust, sweat, the city's earthiness, fills your nostrils. Roman soldiers line the road, their dust-covered armour and large shields give them an imposing presence, as they watch the crowd. Then, you see Him.

Jesus, beaten and covered in blood and dust, walks barefoot, a crown of thorns pressed into His head. He is dragging the weight of a large wooden cross. Even amidst the noise, you can hear the hard wood scraping against the cobblestones. Suddenly, He stumbles. The crowd erupts, some laugh and jeer cruelly, while others cry out in grief. Frustrated, a Roman soldier strikes Jesus with a stick. You can almost feel the impact. Then, out of nowhere, a Roman grabs you roughly from the crowd. You must carry the cross.

The weight is immense. The hard wood digs into your shoulder as you drag it forward. You watch Jesus ahead of you, He stumbles with exhaustion, yet keeps walking. The crowd's jeers and insults, once directed only at Him, now fall upon you as well. Though you are innocent, you are treated as guilty by association.

With each painful step, frustration builds in you. You have done nothing wrong, yet you bear the weight of this burden. Anger flickers in your heart, anger at Jesus, at the soldiers, at the unfairness of it all. Why must you suffer? Finally, you reach the top of the hill. You drop the cross, your breath heavy, sweat dripping from your face. You look up at Jesus. He is battered, broken, and in unimaginable pain, yet He looks at you with love. In His suffering, all that matter is you.

He asks you, **"Are you okay?"** Reflect on this question. **Are you okay?** Even in His agony, Jesus's love for you remains unwavering, while you are suffering with your own cross.

The soldiers seize Jesus, laying Him upon the cross. With each hammer strike, the nails are driven into His hands and feet, breathe deeply. Let yourself feel the weight of His sacrifice. As they lift Him up, you stand before Him. Most of the crowd has dispersed, their interest fading. Yet, among the few who remain, you see Mary. Her face is pale, her heart breaking as she watches her Son suffer. His blood drips from the wounds, His bruises turn dark, His body trembling in pain. Yet, He does not curse His tormentors. Instead, He speaks:

(Luke 23:34) *"Father, forgive them, for they know not what they do."*

Reflection

Now that the meditation has ended, take a few moments in silence. Reflect on what God might be speaking to your heart through this experience. What emotions did you feel? What did Jesus' gaze say to you? What does His suffering mean for your life?

Closing Prayer

Lord Jesus, thank You for allowing me to walk with You on this journey. In Your suffering, You revealed the depth of Your love. Help me to carry my own cross with faith, knowing that You are always beside me. May this meditation deepen my love for You and transform my heart to be more like Yours.

Amen.

Finding God in the Wilderness

A Journey Through Spiritual Desolation to Divine Encounter

Heavenly Father, the wilderness is a place where we feel distant from You, a place where our sins have led us to wander, lost and alone. Yet even in this desolation, I seek You. I seek Your Spirit, the Light in the darkness, to guide my steps and lead me on the path that Christ, our Savior, has already walked before me. I wait for You in this stillness. I do not need to strive or search, Your light is already here. All I must do is open my eyes to see, and surrender this moment to You, Lord. Guide my mind, my breath, my body, and my spirit. Let me be still.

Amen.

Psalm 46:10 — *"Be still, and know that I am God."*

What is the Wilderness?

I further expanded the idea of the spiritual wilderness that St Teresa of Avila created, as a way to understand in simple terms the spiritual path of all Christians. I used this framework to help keep me heading in the right direction, and through this small book I hope it can do the same for you.

To describe what is this wilderness, it is a place of spiritual death where we are cut off from the Father. We were born to this wilderness due to the disobedience of Adam and Eve in the beginning, and continue to exist here due to our own disobedience and ignorance. The wilderness is made up of sin, demons, temptations and human arrogance, that will do everything possible to pull us further away from the Father. While the wilderness is a terrible place, where we suffer, there is hope. Through the gift of grace, we are capable of using the suffering, the isolation to change for the better, we do this by not looking at ourselves but by looking at God and others. Just as the Israelites had to suffer in the wilderness, and Jesus who suffered 40 days in the wilderness to empathize the reliance on the Father, more than food and water. While the wilderness is a terrible place, it is necessary.

Guided Meditation, Encounter in the Wilderness

Prayer

Come, Holy Spirit, guide my thoughts toward a meeting of my heart and Yours, to bring me closer to Jesus in Your power as I travel to the Father. Amen.

The Wilderness

Imagine being in the spiritual wilderness, a place where we all begin, away from God, stumbling in the darkness, lost and alone. You walk along a narrow path, surrounded by hollow, dead trees. The air is heavy, thick with silence, as the encroaching, oppressive darkness reaches for you. The path beneath your feet is uneven and treacherous. You slip and stumble. And before you even realize what has happened, you have lost the path. Yet, you tell yourself, *I can do this*. You have strength, intelligence, and great fortitude. Push forward, convinced you do not need help. But the wilderness and your mind are alike, both lost, both believing they can navigate on their own. Stop. Take a breath. Look

13

around. Can you still see the path? Were you ever sure there was a path? It's okay. Just breathe. Admit to yourself that you do not know where you are or where you are going.

If you truly want to find Christ, you must first humble yourself and admit you need help. If you refuse, your lack of humility will cause you to walk alone. But I want you to say it, not just in your mind, but in your heart:

"I need help."

"I cannot do this alone."

"God, guide me."

This is the beginning of real humility, to surrender control and finally understand what it means to trust God. Just take a moment and focus on that surrender.

For a long time, you have walked alone. But now pause. Listen. Can you hear it? A voice, gentle yet steady, calling your name, not with anger, not with judgment, but with longing. It has always been calling, but only now, in surrender, do you truly hear it. Like the father of the prodigal son, God has never stopped watching for you, waiting, loving you. He calls you, he wants you to come home.

Now, feel it. A warmth begins to stir in your chest, a light, gentle but steady. It is responding to your need for help, a balm for your suffering soul. That is God. You were never truly alone. Through all your wandering, through all your fears, through every wrong turn, he was always with you. For a few moments, I want you to just rest in that truth. This journey was never meant to be under taken alone, you do this with God, in the name of Jesus, with the power of the Spirit.

Reflection

Now that the meditation has ended, take a few moments in silence. Reflect on what God might be speaking to your heart through this experience. What does it mean to really surrender your will to Gods?

Closing Prayer

Holy spirit, thank you for being with me through this meditation, for revealing what is needed and the journey that is still to come. I will continue to walk this path, to follow in the footsteps of Jesus as I make the journey back home. Amen

To Walk the Narrow Path

The Light of God will Light the Way

Opening Prayer

Come, Holy Spirit, bring Your light and keep back the shadows of sin and vain illusion, as I walk the narrow path of the soul. Quiet my thoughts of fear and doubt, for my heart is so easily led astray. With each step forward, I remember the sacrifice of my Lord, whose name is forever on my lips. Grant me, a desperate soul, the strength to pass through the great desolation and reach union with You, the pure Light, the source of all things. Father, Abba, I am coming home. Amen.

Luke 15:20 - *"But while he was still a long way off, his father saw him and was filled with compassion; he ran to his son, threw his arms around him and kissed him."*

Guided Meditation – Going Home

We will begin the meditation by taking a few moments to become gratefully aware of the Spirit of God, His Holy Spirit indwelling in our soul. Feel His warmth within you, like a quiet fire that refuses to be extinguished. Let its radiance push back the darkness, revealing the truth of where you stand. You begin to see more clearly, the spiritual wilderness around you, the daunting reality of where you are. The invisible eyes watch from behind the shadows, but they have no power over you. The Spirit is with you, and you are never alone. It would be easy to stay where you are, afraid of the narrow path now visible before you, the path the Spirit calls you to take between bending trees, dry rocks, and dead things. But you have come this far. Now, as Christ did, take up your cross. Do not wait for another to do it for you. The Spirit calls you forward.

Walk the long path. Now that you are walking in the footsteps of Christ, keep your mind on the Spirit, on Jesus. Your past will whisper, calling you to turn back. But the Spirit calls you forward. When you stumble, He does not condemn you, He lifts you up.

You are walking in the footsteps of Christ, carrying the cross just as He did, with only love in your heart. Many have come before you, walking this same path through the wilderness. Temptations rise from the darkest places of your mind, trying to pull you away. But God believes in you. He chose you before you were even born, and knew you could do this. Each time you fall, each time you lose faith, it is okay. God does not expect you to move perfectly, without fault or mistake. Get back to your feet and, regardless of what the world tells you, march forward without looking back. For what is waiting for you is greater than anything in creation.

As the wilderness and the darkness fade, you see the City of God on top of the hill, glowing like a bright star with towering walls. For the first time, the darkness of sin loses its grip on you as you draw closer to the great gates of the city. The weight you carried, the fears, the burdens, they lose their hold. You are no longer a prisoner of darkness; you are a child walking home.

Lay everything before the Father, your struggles, your victories, your very self. Nothing is yours alone; all belongs to Him. Now, rest at the gate in peace. The journey has been long, but you are finally here. You do not need to beg or demand entrance, for the Father has always been waiting. He has watched you from the moment you were born. And now you are home.

Reflection

Now that the meditation has ended, take a few moments in silence. Reflect on what it means to be with the Father, what he wants and how we reach him.

Closing Prayer

Father, I know the journey is long, for the path of the spirit is full of struggle and hard work, but you are the light at the other side, the great love that we are missing. I will keep on going till I make it.

Amen

Final Reflection:

The spiritual journey for all who walk, can feel dry at times. Many times, God seems distant, a great unknown we are told to love. I knew the stories of Christ from the Bible having being taught them as a child, and I understood His importance, yet this intellectual understanding left me feeling like something was missing. I wanted more. It was not enough for me to just read about Jesus as if He were just a figure from history. To truly appreciate the depth of His sacrifice and love, I needed more, otherwise, I would be blown from one convincing idea to another.

I was introduced to the idea of imaginative prayer during my extensive research into Christian practices, but it took a long time for me to truly grasp what it meant, let alone how best to practice it. Fortunately, I already had a background in meditations from other traditions, a skill that served me well. With guidance from a Catholic deacon, I began researching deeper ways to pray, deeper ways to understand Scripture, and deeper ways to place myself within the Gospel stories For my first serious attempt, I chose the Passion of Christ, the same meditation I guided you through in this book, I took on the role of Simon of Cyrene. I positioned myself within the scene, becoming both an observer and a participant. I built a vivid world in my mind, the smells, the noises, the heat of the sun and roughness of the wooden cross. The experience was overwhelming.

As I carried the cross behind Christ, I became painfully aware of my own suffering, my own struggles. But something even deeper was revealed, my selfishness, my frustration, my resistance to suffering. It was as though my heart was being held up to a mirror, exposing the parts of me I often ignored. And yet, at the end of my meditation, despite His suffering, despite the unimaginable pain He bore, Christ turned to me, showing his concern for us with a few, simple words *"Are you okay?"* Thae same question I wanted you to consider during your meditation.

I had spent so much time thinking about my struggles, my burdens and traumas that the idea of being more concerned about someone else was a hard pill to swallow. And yet, here was Christ, enduring the unthinkable, and His concern was still for me. For us. For you.

I left that meditation with the beginnings of serious, personal change. The Passion was no longer just a story, it became a lived experience that I would spend many weeks meditating on. I realized that Jesus isn't distant. His suffering is not just a historical event. He invites each of us to walk with Him, to bear the cross, not out of obligation, but out of love. And in that journey, we don't walk alone. He carries it with us.

To those who pick up this book and step into these meditations, my hope is that you open your heart fully to the experience and allow it to change you. Every journey is different, and some moments may feel more powerful than others. But know that God is always there, waiting for you. He does not force you to carry the cross, nor does He demand perfection. But He does call you to walk with Him.

John 10:27-28 – *"My sheep listen to my voice; I know them, and they follow me. I give them eternal life, and they shall never perish; no one will snatch them out of my hand."*

Printed in Great Britain
by Amazon

61530820R00020